Y0-BGE-524

¡FIESTA!
PUBLICATIONS

VIDA MARINA SEA LIFE

Take your students on a voyage of learning!

This book brings the world of sea life into your classroom

using fun and interesting projects that teach about

creatures that live in and around the ocean.

Welcome to VIDA MARINA/SEA LIFE!
This book provides you with bilingual materials to teach a fun
and comprehensive unit on SEA LIFE. Included is a teacher's
instruction section with details for each project along with ideas
you can use throughout your classroom. Discover SEA LIFE
using skills in reading, math, spelling, and art. Contains both
Spanish and English versions of each project in one book!

VISIT: WWW.FIESTAPUBLICATIONS.COM

ISBN 0-9755939-7-8

Printed in the United States of America

Flashcards

Using pictures and names of sea life.

shark

The various sea life manipulatives can be used in several ways to create fun and interesting learning flashcards.

Copy and cut desired manipulatives onto construction paper or card stock. Laminate cards for permanent use in classroom or make sets for each student for a take-home project.

Use transparencies on an overhead for classroom discussions and in centers.

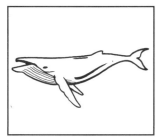

whale

Concentration

crab

This ever popular game helps children develop memory and matching skills. Best when played in small groups.

There are several variations of "Sea Life Concentration" that you can try.

Younger students match picture card to same picture card. Advance difficulty by mixing and matching combinations - i.e.: picture card with sea animal will match picture card with the same sea animal name.

ASSEMBLY INSTRUCTIONS
Copy and cut desired manipulatives onto construction paper or card stock. Laminate cards for permanent use.

HOW TO PLAY
1. Mix up cards and lay them upside down in rows.
2. Students take turns choosing two cards at a time. If they choose two cards that are a match, they get another turn. If there is no match, the next player gets a turn. The player with the most matched pairs wins the game!

Sea Life Mobiles

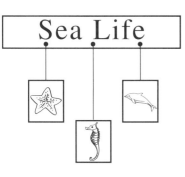

A fun art project that reinforces the SEA LIFE unit. Use as a classroom decoration or to identify centers that focus on specific groups.

ASSEMBLY INSTRUCTIONS
Select a "header card" for your mobile. Copy onto construction paper, fold and punch holes as necessary. Use string, fishline or dental floss to connect manipulatives to header. Hang from ceiling or walls.

Have students color their mobile pieces. Use crayons, paint, markers, or glitter.

My Sea Life Book

Students create and color their own "Sea Life" book. Teachers can design books by choosing various pages.

Students can write stories or facts about the sea and sea life.

Have students share their finished books with the class. These books make a great take home project. Have your students complete several books to create their own "My Sea Life" library!

Finished books make an excellent bulletin board theme.

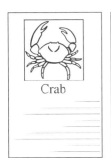

Crab

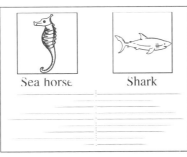

Sea horse   Shark

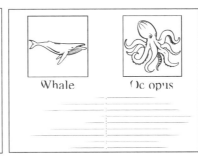

Whale   Octopus

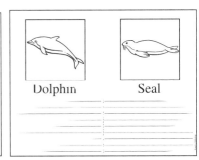

Dolphin   Seal

My Sea Life Number Book

This book is a fun and interesting way to integrate sea life and counting!

Have students color and assemble book, or copy each page onto colored card stock and laminate for permanent use.

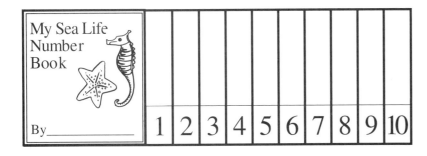

Venn Diagrams

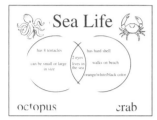

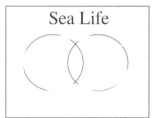

We have provided you with venn diagram blacklines. Use these as an overhead transparency to aid in classroom discussions or give one to each student to fill out. This is an excellent project to learn the differences and similarities of sea life and assess your student's listening and comprehension skills.

Sentence Strips and Vocabulary Cards

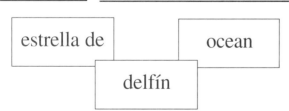

The sentence strips and vocabulary cards reinforce the basic concepts found throughout this unit. Use in several ways; on bulletin boards, in centers, pocket charts and as examples for story starter books.

I Know About Sea Life Certificate

This is a great way to recognize and reward your students as they progress through this unit.

Use as a specific incentive when students finish a defined list of projects or as a general award when the unit is complete. These make a great classroom bulletin board theme and provide students a take home diploma they can be proud of.

Let students color their own certificate as a classroom art project or copy on colored paper.

Dear Parents Letter

Send this note home with students to let their parents know what's going on in their classroom. Provides an introduction to parents of the upcoming unit.

Bulletin Board Ideas

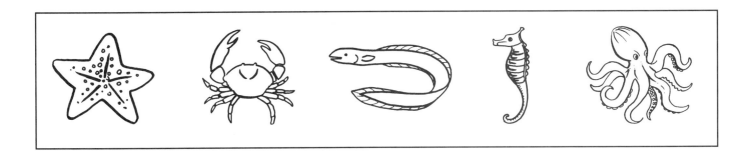

- Use the bulletin board strips to make all types of sea life borders. Create specific borders such as a sea animal board. Have each student color corresponding pictures to use on the board.

- Make a story starter board using inside book pages – some suggested themes: "My Favorite Sea Animal" or "Things I Know About the Sea."

- Have students make collages from magazines featuring all types of sea life.

- Use Venn Diagrams, worksheets, book covers and flashcard masters to create a wide variety of sea life bulletin boards.

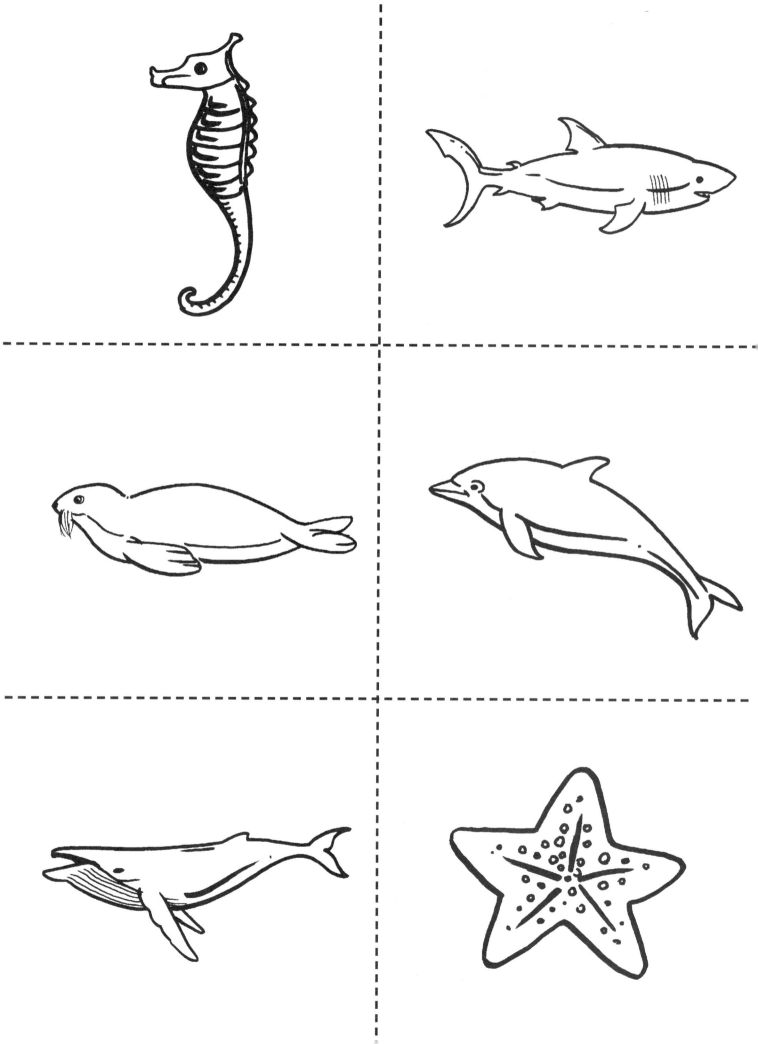

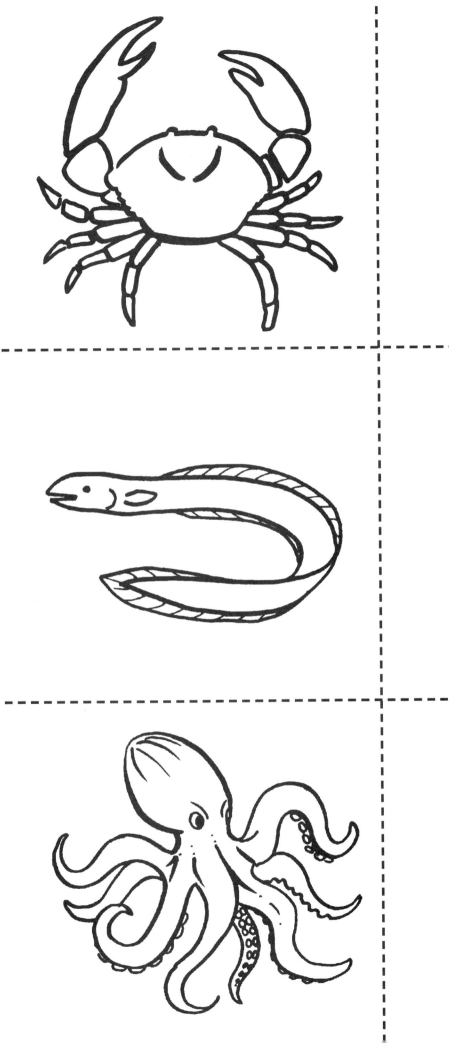

tiburón	caballito de mar
delfín	foca
estrella de mar	ballena

shark	sea horse
dolphin	seal
starfish	whale

cangrejo

anguila

pulpo

crab

eel

octopus

Móviles de vida marina

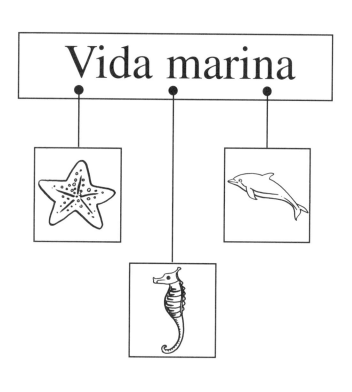

Vida marina

Kingsley Publishing

Vida marina

Vida marina

Sea Life Mobiles

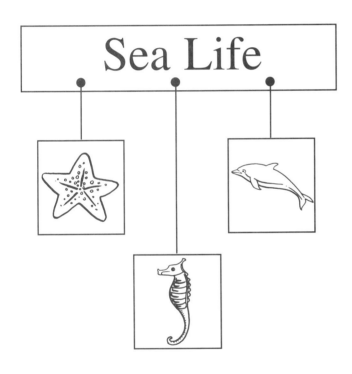

Sea Life

Sea Life

Sea Life

Kingsley Publishing

caballito de mar

tiburón

foca

delfín

ballena

estrella de mar

cangrejo

pulpo

anguila

sea horse | shark | seal

dolphin | whale | starfish

crab | octopus | eel

Kingsley Publishing

Nombre:

Este libro es de

Sé de la vida marina

This Book
Created By

Name: _____

I Know About Sea Life

Caballito de mar

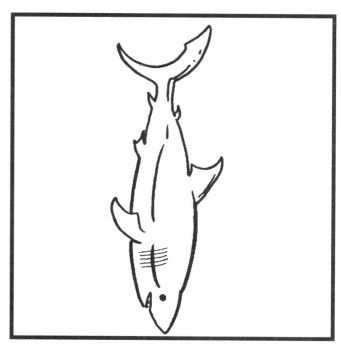

Tiburón

Sea horse

Shark

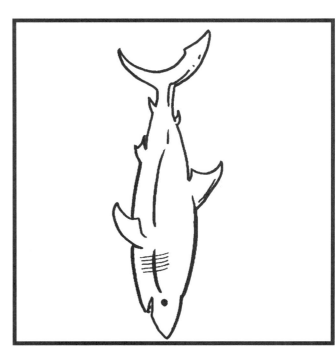

Ballena

Pulpo

Whale

Octopus

Delfín

Foca

Dolphin

Seal

Cangrejo

Estrella de mar

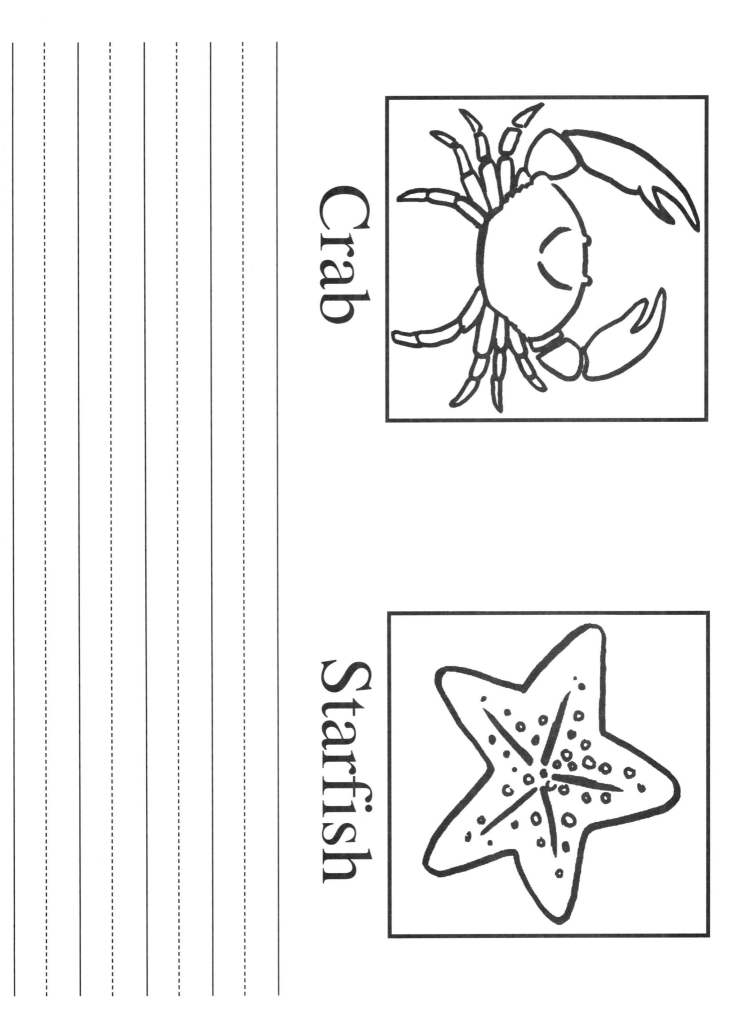

Crab

Starfish

Anguila

Eel

Mi libro de vida marina

Por _____

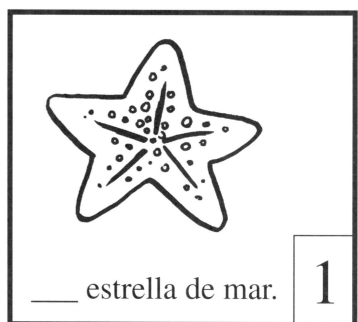

____ estrella de mar.

1

____ delfines.

2

____ cangrejos.

3

My Sea Life Number Book

By _____

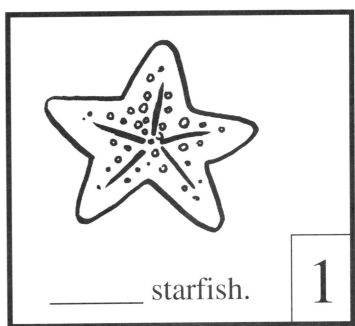

_____ starfish.

1

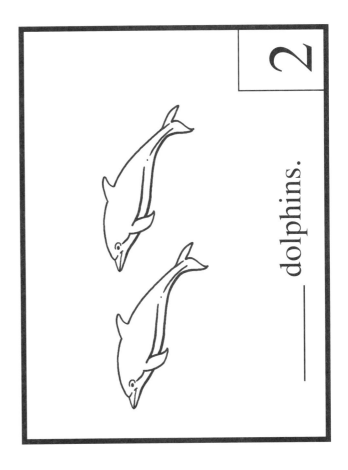

_____ dolphins.

2

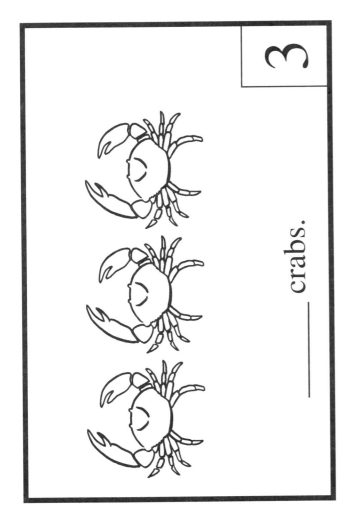

_____ crabs.

3

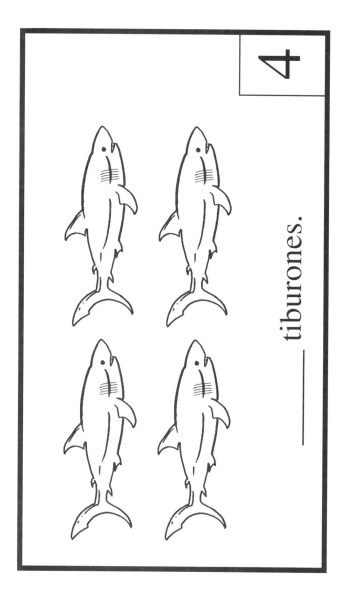

_____ tiburones.

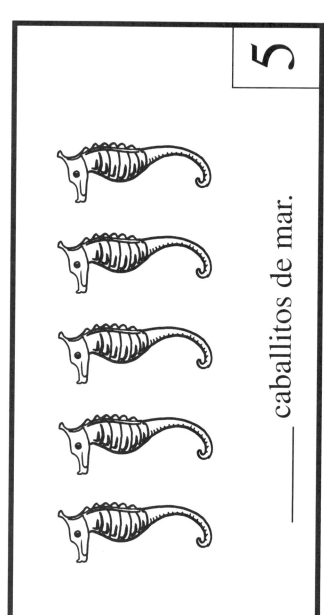

_____ caballitos de mar.

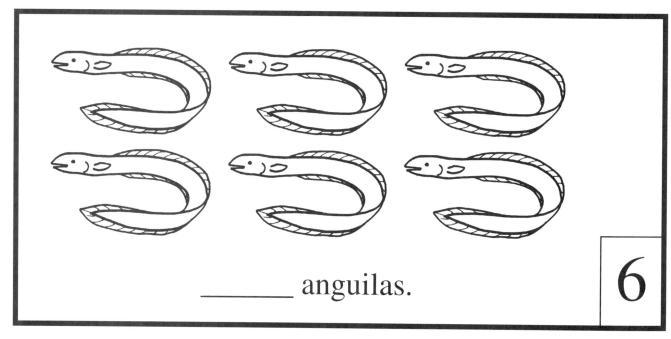

_____ anguilas.

4

_____ sharks.

5

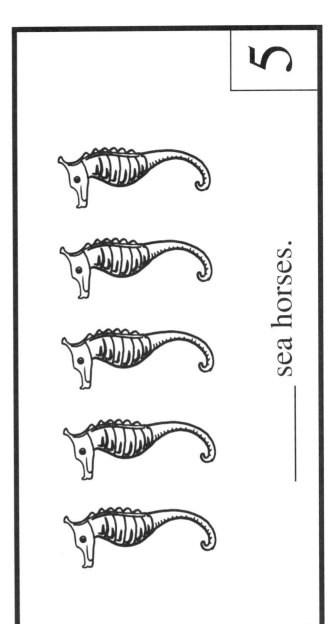

_____ sea horses.

6

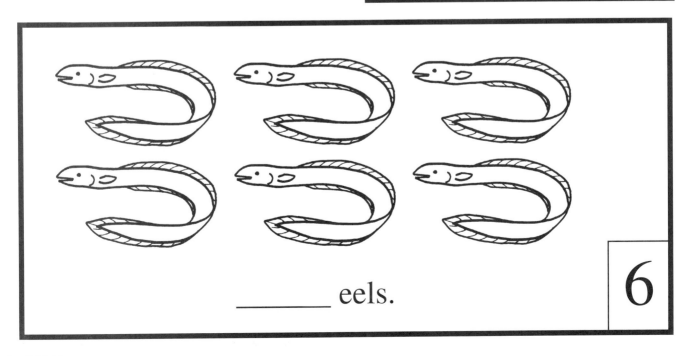

_____ eels.

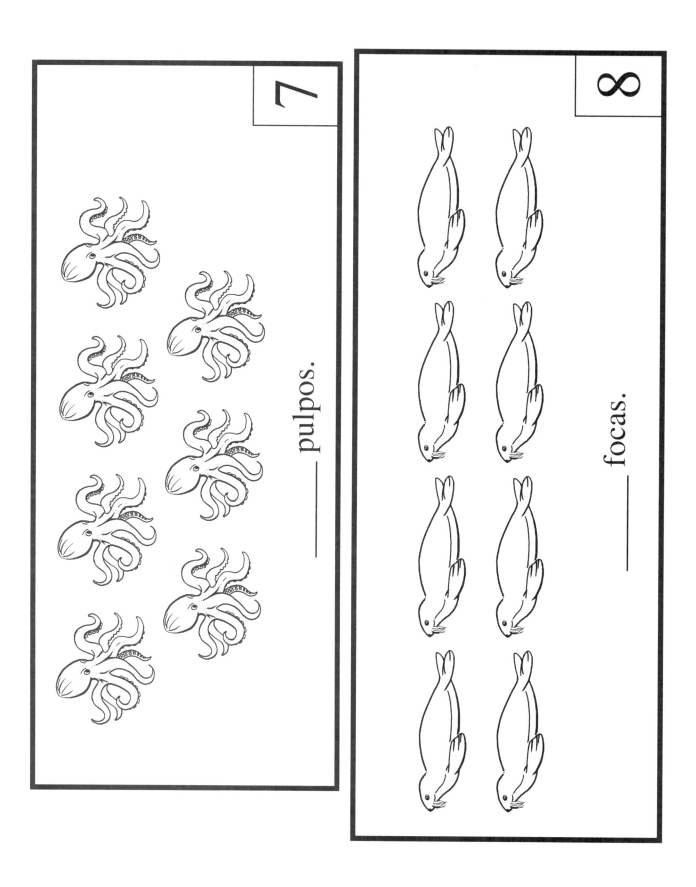

7

——— pulpos.

8

——— focas.

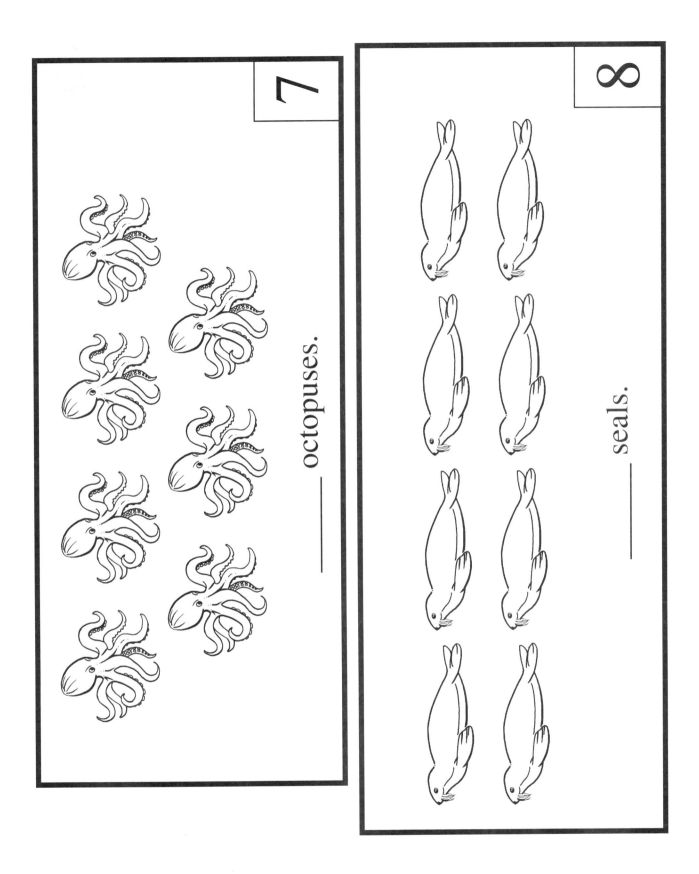

7

_____ octopuses.

8

_____ seals.

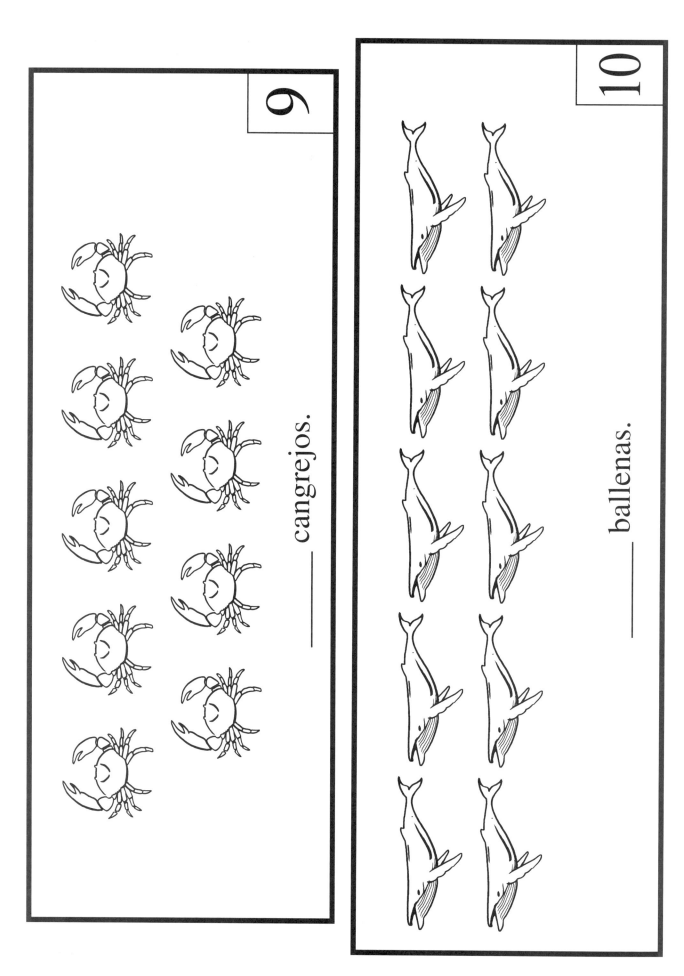

9

_____ cangrejos.

10

_____ ballenas.

9

_____ crabs.

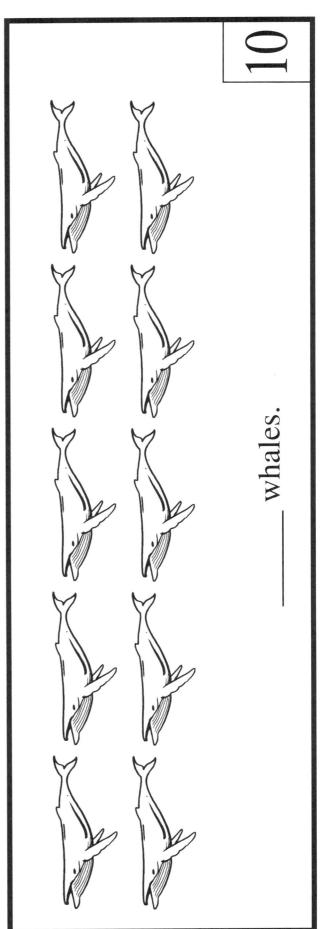

10

_____ whales.

Vida marina

pulpo

cangrejo

pulpo
- tiene 8 tentáculos
- pertenece a un grupo de animales marinos llamados moluscos

(intersección)
- 2 ojos
- vive en el mar

cangrejo
- tiene un caparazón duro
- corre por la playa
- anaranjado/blanco/negro

Sea Life

octopus

crab

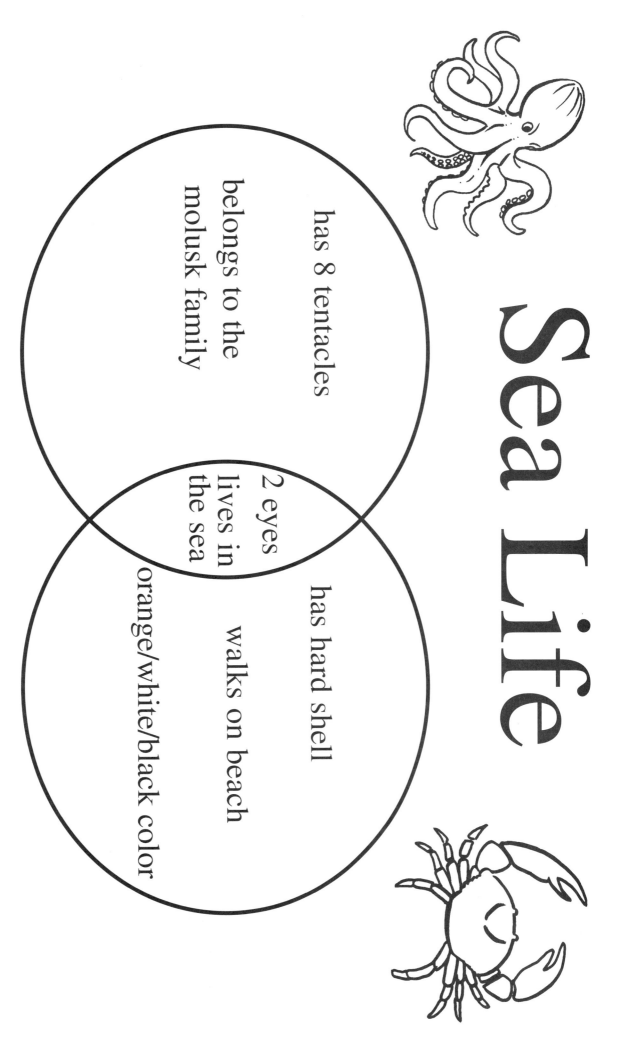

- has 8 tentacles
- belongs to the molusk family

- 2 eyes
- lives in the sea

- has hard shell
- walks on beach
- orange/white/black color

Vida marina

_____

_____

_____

_____

Sea Life

Muchas plantas y animales viven en el mar.

Algunos animales marinos

Many plants and animals live in the sea.

Some sea animals

tienen conchas.

pueden respirar bajo el agua.

pasan tiempo en la arena.

have shells.

have fins.

can breath underwater.

spend time on the sand.

son mamíferos.

nos dan alimentos

para comer. tienen aletas.

are mammals.

provide food for

us to eat.

anguila

ballena

foca

estrella de mar

tiburón

delfín

seal

whale

eel

dolphin

shark

starfish

caballito de mar	pulpo	cangrejo
océano	playa	marea

crab

octopus

sea horse

tide

beach

ocean

CERTIFICADO

Nombre: _____

¡Felicidades!
Ya eres un experto de
nuestra vida marina!

¡Yo sé
de vida
marina!

Kingsley Publishing

CERTIFICATE

Sea Life

Name: _____

Congratulations!
You are now an
expert on
sea life!

I Know
About Sea
Life!

Estimados padres,

Empezamos una unidad sobre la vida marina. Aprenderemos mucho acerca de los animales marinos.

Por favor únanse a nosotros e incluyan conversaciones en casa acerca del mar, a diario. Incluyan experiencias que hayan tenido acerca del mar, en sus pláticas.

Cuando visiten la biblioteca pública, ayuden a sus hijos a buscar libros informativos acerca de los animales marinos.

Conversaciones familiares ayudan a aprender conceptos que se estudian en clase.

Sinceramente,

Dear Parents,

We are starting a unit on SEA LIFE. We will be learning about the sea and sea animals.

Please join us by including daily conversations about the sea at home. Include in your discussions any sea experiences you may have had.

When visiting the public library look for books about the sea and sea animals for your child.

Family discussions will help reinforce concepts being learned in class!

Sincerely,

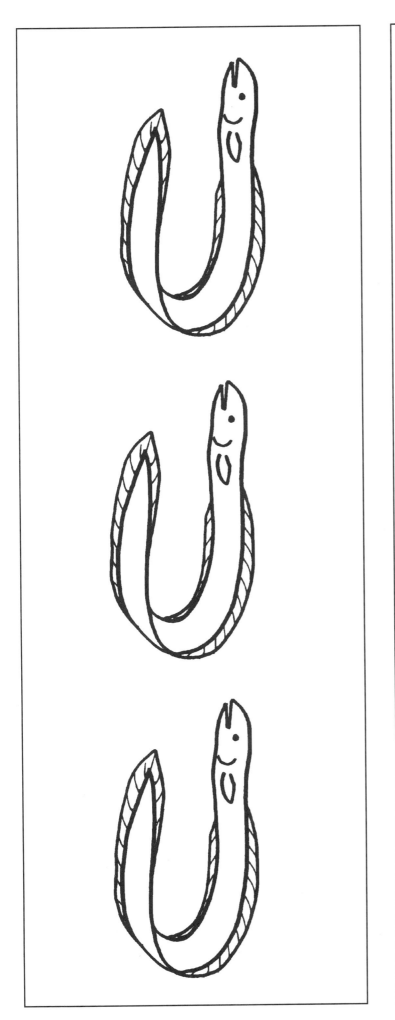

Nombre:_____

El pulpo

Lee el párrafo.
Responde las preguntas.
Colorea el dibujo.

El pulpo tiene ocho brazos que se llaman tentáculos. Esos tentáculos se utilizan para moverse y agarrar alimentos. Los pulpos pertenecen a un grupo de animales marinos llamados moluscos. Otros moluscos son el calamar, la almeja y la ostra. Los moluscos tienen cuerpos blandos sin huesos. Algunos moluscos tienen conchas, otros no.

1. El pulpo tiene diez tentáculos. (Haz un círculo)

   cierto   falso

2. ¿Tienen conchas los pulpos ? (Haz un círculo)

   sí   no

3. El pulpo es un _____. (Haz un círculo)

   pez   molusco

4 El pulpo utiliza sus tentáculos para____. (Haz un círculo)

   agarrar alimentos   caminar por la playa

5. Todos los moluscos tienen _____ . (Haz un círculo)

   huesos   cuerpos blandos

EXTRA:
¿Cómo se llaman los brazos de un pulpo?   _____.

Name:_____

Octopus

Read the story below.
Answer the questions.
Color the picture.

An octopus has eight arms, called tentacles. It uses its tentacles to move and catch food. Octopuses belong to a sea life family called mollusks. Some other mollusks are squid, clams and oysters. Mollusks have soft bodies without bones. Some mollusks have shells, some do not.

1. An octopus has ten tentacles. (Circle one)

    true   false

2. Does an octopus have a shell? (Circle one)

    yes   no

3. An octopus is a _____. (Circle one)

    fish   mollusk

4. An octopus uses its tentacles to _____. (Circle one)

    catch food   walk on the beach

5. All mollusks have _____ . (Circle one)

    bones   soft bodies

BONUS:

What are the arms of an octopus called? _____.

Nombre:_____

El caballito de mar

Lee el párrafo.
Responde las preguntas.
Colorea el dibujo.

   Este es un caballito de mar. El caballito de mar tiene aletas y agallas. Utiliza sus aletas para moverse y sus agallas para respirar. Los caballitos de mar pueden respirar dentro del agua. La mayoría de los caballitos de mar son pequeños, de tres a seis pulgadas de largo. La mayoría de los caballitos de mar viven en aguas templadas.

1. El caballito de mar es generalmente muy grande.
   (Haz un círculo)   cierto   falso
2. El caballito de mar utiliza sus agallas para_____ bajo el agua. (Haz un círculo)   respirar   hablar
3. El caballito de mar no tiene aletas.
   (Haz un círculo)   cierto   falso
4. La mayoría de los caballitos de mar viven en aguas _____. (Haz un círculo)   frías   templadas

EXTRA:

1. Subraya la primera palabra en cada oración del párrafo anterior.
2. Haz un círculo alrededor de cada punto en el párrafo anterior.
3. ¿Cuántas veces puedes encontrar la palabra "la" en el párrafo anterior? _____.

Name:_____

Sea Horse

Read the story below.
Answer the questions.
Color the picture.

    This is a sea horse. A sea horse has fins
and gills. It uses its fins to move and
its gills to breathe. Sea horses can breathe
under the water. Most sea horses are small,
from three to six inches long.
Most sea horses live in warm water.

1. A sea horse is usually very large. (Circle one)
       true   false
2. A sea horse uses its gills to_____under water.
  (Circle one)   breathe   talk
3. A sea horse does not have fins. (Circle one)
       true   false
4. Most sea horses live in _____water. (Circle one)
      cold   warm

BONUS:
1. Underline the first word in each sentence in the
    paragraph above.
2. Circle all the periods in the paragraph above.
3. How many times can you find the word "to" in the
    paragraph above? _____.

Nombre:_____

La estrella de mar

Lee el párrafo.
Responde las preguntas.
Colorea el dibujo.

La estrella de mar generalmente tiene cinco tentáculos, pero puede tener más. En la parte de abajo de sus tentáculos hay ventosas que las estrellas de mar utilizan para moverse de un lugar a otro y para conseguir sus alimentos. La boca de la estrellas de mar está en el centro, abajo de su cuerpo. La estrella de mar tiene piel áspera y llena de espinitas.

1. Todas las estrellas de mar tienen cinco tentáculos.
   (Haz un círculo)   cierto   falso

2. La estrella de mar utiliza sus ventosas para _____.
   (Haz un círculo)   moverse y comer   cantar y bailar

3. La estrella de mar no tiene boca.   (Haz un círculo)
          cierto   falso

4. La estrella de mar tiene la piel _____ . (Haz un círculo)
          lisa   áspera

EXTRA:

1. ¿Cuántos sustantivos hay en el párrafo anterior?_____.

2. Subraya la penúltima palabra de cada oración
   del párrafo anterior.

3. Haz un círculo alrededor de todos los verbos en el
   párrafo anterior.

Name:_____

Starfish

Read the story below.
Answer the questions.
Color the picture.

A starfish usually has five arms, but can have more. The bottom side of their arms have suckers which the starfish uses to move around and get its food. A starfish's mouth is in the center on its underside. Starfish have spiny and rough skin.

1. A starfish always has five arms. (Circle one)

    true   false

2. Starfish use their suckers to _____. (Circle one)

    move and eat   sing and dance

3. Starfish do not have mouths. (Circle one)

    true   false

4. A starfish has _____ skin. (Circle one)

    smooth   rough

BONUS:

1. How many nouns do you find in the paragraph above?_____.

2. Underline the second from the last word in each sentence in the paragraph above.

3. Circle all the verbs in the paragraph above.

Nombre:_____

La foca

Lee el párrafo.
Responde las preguntas.
Colorea el dibujo

Este dibujo es de una foca. Focas son animales que viven en el mar y que tienen piel. Las focas nadan muy bien, aunque pasan tiem- po en tierra firme. La foca vive en el mar durante muchos meses, pero pare sus crías en la playa. Para respirar aire, la foca sube a la superficie del agua.

1. Las focas pueden respirar dentro del agua.
    (Haz un círculo)   cierto   falso
2. Las focas pueden vivir en el mar o en tierra firme.
    (Haz un círculo)   cierto   falso
3. Las focas _____ muy bien.   (Haz un círculo)
         corren   nadan
4. Las focas no tienen piel.   (Haz un círculo)
         cierto   falso

EXTRA:
1. ¿Cuántas veces encuentras la palabra "en" en el párrafo anterior? _____.
2. ¿Cuántas veces encuentras la palabra "foca" en el párrafo anterior? _____.
3. Haz un círculo alrededor de la tercera palabra en cada oración del párrafo anterior.

Name:_____

Seal

Read the story below.
Answer the questions.
Color the picture.

   This is a seal. Seals are animals
that live in the sea and have fur.
Seals are very good swimmers,
but also spend time on the land.
A seal will spend many months at a time in the sea, but has its
babies on the beach. To breathe, a seal comes to the surface.

1. Seals can breathe under the water. (Circle one)
      true   false
2. Seals can live in the sea or on land. (Circle one)
      true   false
3. Seals are very good_____. (Circle one)
      joggers   swimmers
4. Seals do not have fur. (Circle one)
      true   false

BONUS:
1. How many times do you find the word "in" in the
   paragraph above?_____.
2. How many times do you find the word "seal" in the
   paragraph above?_____.
3. Circle the third word in each sentence in the
   paragraph above.

Nombre:_____

La ballena

Lee el párrafo.
Responde las preguntas.
Colorea el dibujo

Las ballenas siempre viven en el mar. La ballena respira aire. Para eso, sube a la superficie del mar donde exhala el aire que queda en sus pulmones. Cuando se mantienen dentro del agua, cesan de respirar. Las ballenas son mamíferos como los seres humanos. También pertenecen a la familia de las focas, morsas y leones marinos.

1. Las ballenas respiran dentro del agua. (Haz un círculo)

    cierto   falso

2. Las ballenas pertenecen a la familia de los _____.

    (Haz un círculo)   cangrejos   leones marinos

3. Las ballenas son _____ como los seres humanos.

    (Haz un círculo)   mamíferos   moluscos

4. Las ballenas exhalan aire _____.

    (Haz un círculo)

    en el fondo del mar   en la superficie del mar

EXTRA:

1. ¿Cuántos sustantivos encuentras en el párrafo anterior?

2. ¿Cuántas veces se ha usado la letra "t" como primera letra de palabra en el párrafo anterior?

3. Haz un círculo alrededor de cada punto en el párrafo anterior.

Name:_____

Whale

Read the story below.
Answer the questions.
Color the picture.

Whales live in the water at all times. A whale breathes by coming to the surface of the water to exhale air from its lungs. While under water, they hold their breath. Whales are mammals, like humans. They are related to seals, walruses and sea lions.

1. Whales breathe underwater. (Circle one)

      true   false

2. Whales are related to _____. (Circle one.

      crabs   sea lions

3. Whales are _____like humans. (Circle one)

      mammals   mollusks

4. Whales exhale air _____. (Circle one)

      under water   on the surface

BONUS:

1. How many nouns do you find in the paragraph above?_____

2. How many times is the letter "t" used as the first letter in a word in the paragraph above? _____

3. Circle each period in the paragraph above.

Nombre:_____

El cangrejo

Lee el párrafo.
Responde las preguntas.
Colorea el dibujo.

Los cangrejos tienen diez patas y dos de ellas son pinzas. Hay muchos tipos de cangrejos. Algunos viven en el océano, otros en huecos en la arena. Los cangrejos pueden caminar hacia adelante, hacia atrás, o de lado. Los cangrejos generalmente tienen caparazones duros que cubren sus cuerpos.

1. Los cangrejos tienen _____ patas. (Haz un círculo)

  dos   diez

2. Los cangrejos pueden caminar de lado. (Haz un círculo)

  cierto   falso

3. Los cangrejos siempre viven en el océano. (Haz un círculo)   cierto   falso

4. Los cangrejos pueden vivir en _____. (Haz un círculo)   la arena   el árbol

EXTRA:

1. ¿Cuántos verbos hay en el párrafo anterior? _____.

2. Haz un círculo alrededor de cada segunda palabra en cada oración.

3. Subraya cada sustantivo en el párrafo anterior.

Name:_____

Crab

Read the story below.
Answer the questions.
Color the picture.

Crabs have ten legs, two of them have claws. There are many different types of crabs. Some live in the ocean, some live in holes in the sand. Crabs can walk forwards, backwards, and sideways. Crabs usually have hard shells which cover their bodies.

1. Crabs have _____ legs. (Circle one)

        two   ten

2. Crabs can walk sideways. (Circle one)

        true   false

3. Crabs always live in the ocean. (Circle one)

        true   false

4. Crabs can live in _____. (Circle one)

        the sand   a tree

BONUS:
1. How many verbs are found in the paragraph above?_____.
2. Circle the second word in each sentence.
3. Underline each noun in the paragraph above.

Notes: